This Reading Log Journal belongs to:

_____

HOW TO USE THIS READING LOG JOURNAL?

Harry Potter author J.K. Rowling said: *"If it's a good book, anyone will read it. I'm totally unashamed about still reading things I loved in my childhood."*

Did you know that reading is associated with many benefits?

- It develops your imagination
- It improves your concentration, and
- It improves your language skills

But most importantly: *reading is just a lot of FUN*!

This book review journal allows you to log the most important things and main takeaways from each book you read.

You'll be able to log:

- Author name + book title
- Genre
- Memorable quotes
- Characters
- Plot summary, and
- Star rating

To make sure you'll be able to easily access and reread your book review in the future, add it to the '**Book Overview**' in the beginning.

If you need more space, you'll be able to write additional notes at the end of this journal.

What if you're lacking for inspiration on what books to read?

No need to worry! At the end of this book review notebook, you'll find an overview of 100 Must-Read (fiction) books!

To end with another quote, Taylor Swift once said: *"Books train your mind to imagination to think big."*

With this reading log notebook, you'll be able to train your own mind. And think big. The sky really is the limit…

Happy reading!

Overview of The BOOKS I read

	BOOK TITLE	AUTHOR	PAGE
1			
2			
3			
4			
5			
6			
7			
8			
9			
10			
11			
12			
13			
14			
15			
16			
17			
18			
19			
20			

	BOOK TITLE	AUTHOR	PAGE
21			
22			
23			
24			
25			
26			
27			
28			
29			
30			
31			
32			
33			
34			
35			
36			
37			
38			
39			
40			

	BOOK TITLE	AUTHOR	PAGE
41			
42			
43			
44			
45			
46			
47			
48			
49			
50			
51			
52			
53			
54			
55			
56			
57			
58			
59			
60			

	BOOK TITLE	AUTHOR	PAGE
61			
62			
63			
64			
65			
66			
67			
68			
69			
70			
71			
72			
73			
74			
75			
76			
77			
78			
79			
80			

	BOOK TITLE	AUTHOR	PAGE
81			
82			
83			
84			
85			
86			
87			
88			
89			
90			
91			
92			
93			
94			
95			
96			
97			
98			
99			
100			

EVERY BOOK
- IS A NEW -
WONDERFUL TRAVEL

Book Title

Author _____ Nationality _____

Genre _____ Year _____ Pages _____

Memorable Quote	Page Number

Characters

Plot Summary

Notes

Rating ☆ ☆ ☆ ☆ ☆

Book Title _____

Author _____   Nationality _____

Genre _____   Year _____   Pages _____

Memorable Quote	Page Number

Characters

Plot Summary

Notes

Rating ☆ ☆ ☆ ☆ ☆

Book Title _____

Author _____ Nationality _____

Genre _____ Year _____ Pages _____

Memorable Quote	Page Number

Characters

Plot Summary

Notes

Rating ☆ ☆ ☆ ☆ ☆

Book Title _____

Author _____   Nationality _____

Genre _____   Year _____   Pages _____

Memorable Quote	Page Number

Characters

Plot Summary

Notes

Rating ☆ ☆ ☆ ☆ ☆

Book Title _____

Author _____   Nationality _____

Genre _____   Year _____   Pages _____

Memorable Quote	Page Number

Characters

Plot Summary

Notes

Rating ☆ ☆ ☆ ☆ ☆

Book Title _____

Author _____   Nationality _____

Genre _____   Year _____   Pages _____

Memorable Quote	Page Number

Characters

Plot Summary

Notes

Rating ☆ ☆ ☆ ☆ ☆

Book Title _____

Author _____ Nationality _____

Genre _____ Year _____ Pages _____

Memorable Quote	Page Number

Characters

Plot Summary

Notes

Rating ☆ ☆ ☆ ☆ ☆

Book Title

Author _____ Nationality _____

Genre _____ Year _____ Pages _____

Memorable Quote	Page Number

Characters

Plot Summary

Notes

Rating ☆ ☆ ☆ ☆ ☆

Book Title _____

Author _____   Nationality _____

Genre _____   Year _____   Pages _____

Memorable Quote	Page Number

Characters

Plot Summary

Notes

Rating ☆ ☆ ☆ ☆ ☆

Book Title

Author _____   Nationality _____

Genre _____   Year _____   Pages _____

Memorable Quote	Page Number

Characters

Plot Summary

Notes

Rating ☆ ☆ ☆ ☆ ☆

Book Title _____

Author _____   Nationality _____

Genre _____   Year _____   Pages _____

Memorable Quote	Page Number

Characters

Plot Summary

Notes

Rating ☆ ☆ ☆ ☆ ☆

Book Title _____

Author _____   Nationality _____

Genre _____   Year _____   Pages _____

Memorable Quote	Page Number

Characters

Plot Summary

Notes

Rating ☆ ☆ ☆ ☆ ☆

Book Title _____

Author _____   Nationality _____

Genre _____   Year _____   Pages _____

Memorable Quote	Page Number

Characters

Plot Summary

Notes

Rating ☆ ☆ ☆ ☆ ☆

Book Title

Author _____   Nationality _____

Genre _____   Year _____   Pages _____

Memorable Quote	Page Number

Characters

Plot Summary

Notes

Rating ☆ ☆ ☆ ☆ ☆

Book Title _____

Author _____   Nationality _____

Genre _____   Year _____   Pages _____

Memorable Quote	Page Number

Characters

Plot Summary

Notes

Rating ☆ ☆ ☆ ☆ ☆

Book Title _____

Author _____   Nationality _____

Genre _____   Year _____   Pages _____

Memorable Quote	Page Number

Characters

Plot Summary

Notes

Rating ☆ ☆ ☆ ☆ ☆

Book Title _____

Author _____   Nationality _____

Genre _____   Year _____   Pages _____

Memorable Quote	Page Number

Characters

Plot Summary

Notes

Rating ☆ ☆ ☆ ☆ ☆

Book Title _____

Author _____   Nationality _____

Genre _____   Year _____   Pages _____

Memorable Quote	Page Number

Characters

Plot Summary

Notes

Rating ☆ ☆ ☆ ☆ ☆

Book Title _____

Author _____   Nationality _____

Genre _____   Year _____   Pages _____

Memorable Quote	Page Number

Characters

Plot Summary

Notes

Rating ☆ ☆ ☆ ☆ ☆

Book Title _____

Author _____ Nationality _____

Genre _____ Year _____ Pages _____

Memorable Quote	Page Number

Characters

Plot Summary

Notes

Rating ☆ ☆ ☆ ☆ ☆

Book Title _____

Author _____   Nationality _____

Genre _____   Year _____   Pages _____

Memorable Quote	Page Number

Characters

Plot Summary

Notes

Rating ☆ ☆ ☆ ☆ ☆

Book Title _____

Author _____ Nationality _____

Genre _____ Year _____ Pages _____

Memorable Quote	Page Number

Characters

Plot Summary

Notes

Rating ☆ ☆ ☆ ☆ ☆

Book Title _____

Author _____   Nationality _____

Genre _____   Year _____   Pages _____

Memorable Quote	Page Number

Characters

Plot Summary

Notes

Rating ☆ ☆ ☆ ☆ ☆

Book Title _____

Author _____   Nationality _____

Genre _____   Year _____   Pages _____

Memorable Quote	Page Number

Characters

Plot Summary

Notes

Rating ☆ ☆ ☆ ☆ ☆

Book Title _____

Author _____   Nationality _____

Genre _____   Year _____   Pages _____

Memorable Quote	Page Number

Characters

Plot Summary

Notes

Rating ☆ ☆ ☆ ☆ ☆

Book Title _____

Author _____   Nationality _____

Genre _____   Year _____   Pages _____

Memorable Quote	Page Number

Characters

Plot Summary

Notes

Rating ☆ ☆ ☆ ☆ ☆

Book Title _____

Author _____   Nationality _____

Genre _____   Year _____   Pages _____

Memorable Quote	Page Number

Characters

Plot Summary

Notes

Rating ☆ ☆ ☆ ☆ ☆

Book Title _____

Author _____ Nationality _____

Genre _____ Year _____ Pages _____

Memorable Quote	Page Number

Characters

Plot Summary

Notes

Rating ☆ ☆ ☆ ☆ ☆

Book Title

Author _____ Nationality _____

Genre _____ Year _____ Pages _____

Memorable Quote	Page Number

Characters

Plot Summary

Notes

Rating ☆ ☆ ☆ ☆ ☆

Book Title _____

Author _____ Nationality _____

Genre _____ Year _____ Pages _____

Memorable Quote	Page Number

Characters

Plot Summary

Notes

Rating ☆ ☆ ☆ ☆ ☆

Book Title _____

Author _____   Nationality _____

Genre _____   Year _____   Pages _____

Memorable Quote	Page Number

Characters

Plot Summary

Notes

Rating ☆ ☆ ☆ ☆ ☆

Book Title _____

Author _____ Nationality _____

Genre _____ Year _____ Pages _____

Memorable Quote	Page Number

Characters

Plot Summary

Notes

Rating ☆ ☆ ☆ ☆ ☆

Book Title

Author _____   Nationality _____

Genre _____   Year _____   Pages _____

Memorable Quote	Page Number

Characters

Plot Summary

Notes

Rating ☆ ☆ ☆ ☆ ☆

Book Title _____

Author _____ Nationality _____

Genre _____ Year _____ Pages _____

Memorable Quote	Page Number

Characters

Plot Summary

Notes

Rating ☆ ☆ ☆ ☆ ☆

Book Title _____

Author _____   Nationality _____

Genre _____   Year _____   Pages _____

Memorable Quote	Page Number

Characters

Plot Summary

Notes

Rating ☆ ☆ ☆ ☆ ☆

Book Title _____

Author _____ Nationality _____

Genre _____ Year _____ Pages _____

Memorable Quote	Page Number

Characters

Plot Summary

Notes

Rating ☆ ☆ ☆ ☆ ☆

Book Title _____

Author _____   Nationality _____

Genre _____   Year _____   Pages _____

Memorable Quote	Page Number

Characters

Plot Summary

Notes

Rating ☆ ☆ ☆ ☆ ☆

Book Title

Author _____ Nationality _____

Genre _____ Year _____ Pages _____

Memorable Quote	Page Number

Characters

Plot Summary

Notes

Rating ☆ ☆ ☆ ☆ ☆

Book Title _____

Author _____ Nationality _____

Genre _____ Year _____ Pages _____

Memorable Quote	Page Number

Characters

Plot Summary

Notes

Rating ☆ ☆ ☆ ☆ ☆

Book Title _____

Author _____ Nationality _____

Genre _____ Year _____ Pages _____

Memorable Quote	Page Number

Characters

Plot Summary

Notes

Rating ☆ ☆ ☆ ☆ ☆

Book Title _____

Author _____ Nationality _____

Genre _____ Year _____ Pages _____

Memorable Quote	Page Number

Characters

Plot Summary

Notes

Rating ☆ ☆ ☆ ☆ ☆

Book Title

_____

Author _____   Nationality _____

Genre _____   Year _____   Pages _____

Memorable Quote	Page Number

Characters

Plot Summary

Notes

Rating ☆ ☆ ☆ ☆ ☆

Book Title _____

Author _____   Nationality _____

Genre _____   Year _____   Pages _____

Memorable Quote	Page Number

Characters

Plot Summary

Notes

Rating ☆ ☆ ☆ ☆ ☆

Book Title _____

Author _____   Nationality _____

Genre _____   Year _____   Pages _____

Memorable Quote	Page Number

Characters

Plot Summary

Notes

Rating ☆ ☆ ☆ ☆ ☆

Book Title

Author _____   Nationality _____

Genre _____   Year _____   Pages _____

Memorable Quote	Page Number

Characters

Plot Summary

Notes

Rating ☆ ☆ ☆ ☆ ☆

Book Title _____

Author _____   Nationality _____

Genre _____   Year _____   Pages _____

Memorable Quote	Page Number

Characters

Plot Summary

Notes

Rating ☆ ☆ ☆ ☆ ☆

Book Title

Author _____   Nationality _____

Genre _____   Year _____   Pages _____

Memorable Quote	Page Number

Characters

Plot Summary

Notes

Rating ☆ ☆ ☆ ☆ ☆

Book Title _____

Author _____   Nationality _____

Genre _____   Year _____   Pages _____

Memorable Quote	Page Number

Characters

Plot Summary

Notes

Rating ☆ ☆ ☆ ☆ ☆

Book Title

Author _____   Nationality _____

Genre _____   Year _____   Pages _____

Memorable Quote	Page Number

Characters

Plot Summary

Notes

Rating ☆ ☆ ☆ ☆ ☆

Book Title _____

Author _____   Nationality _____

Genre _____   Year _____   Pages _____

Memorable Quote	Page Number

Characters

Plot Summary

Notes

Rating ☆ ☆ ☆ ☆ ☆

Book Title

Author _____ Nationality _____

Genre _____ Year _____ Pages _____

Memorable Quote	Page Number

Characters

Plot Summary

Notes

Rating ☆ ☆ ☆ ☆ ☆

Book Title _____

Author _____ Nationality _____

Genre _____ Year _____ Pages _____

Memorable Quote	Page Number

Characters

Plot Summary

Notes

Rating ☆ ☆ ☆ ☆ ☆

Book Title _____

Author _____   Nationality _____

Genre _____   Year _____   Pages _____

Memorable Quote	Page Number

Characters

Plot Summary

Notes

Rating ☆ ☆ ☆ ☆ ☆

Book Title _____

Author _____   Nationality _____

Genre _____   Year _____   Pages _____

Memorable Quote	Page Number

Characters

Plot Summary

Notes

Rating ☆ ☆ ☆ ☆ ☆

Book Title

Author _____ Nationality _____

Genre _____ Year _____ Pages _____

Memorable Quote	Page Number

Characters

Plot Summary

Notes

Rating ☆ ☆ ☆ ☆ ☆

Book Title _____

Author _____   Nationality _____

Genre _____   Year _____   Pages _____

Memorable Quote	Page Number

Characters

Plot Summary

Notes

Rating ☆ ☆ ☆ ☆ ☆

Book Title _____

Author _____   Nationality _____

Genre _____   Year _____   Pages _____

Memorable Quote	Page Number

Characters

Plot Summary

Notes

Rating ☆ ☆ ☆ ☆ ☆

Book Title _____

Author _____   Nationality _____

Genre _____   Year _____   Pages _____

Memorable Quote	Page Number

Characters

Plot Summary

Notes

Rating ☆ ☆ ☆ ☆ ☆

Book Title _____

Author _____   Nationality _____

Genre _____   Year _____   Pages _____

Memorable Quote	Page Number

Characters

Plot Summary

Notes

Rating ☆ ☆ ☆ ☆ ☆

Book Title _____

Author _____   Nationality _____

Genre _____   Year _____   Pages _____

Memorable Quote	Page Number

Characters

Plot Summary

Notes

Rating ☆ ☆ ☆ ☆ ☆

Book Title _____

Author _____ Nationality _____

Genre _____ Year _____ Pages _____

Memorable Quote	Page Number

Characters

Plot Summary

Notes

Rating ☆ ☆ ☆ ☆ ☆

Book Title _____

Author _____   Nationality _____

Genre _____   Year _____   Pages _____

Memorable Quote	Page Number

Characters

Plot Summary

Notes

Rating ☆ ☆ ☆ ☆ ☆

Book Title _____

Author _____ Nationality _____

Genre _____ Year _____ Pages _____

Memorable Quote	Page Number

Characters

Plot Summary

Notes

Rating ☆ ☆ ☆ ☆ ☆

Book Title _____

Author _____   Nationality _____

Genre _____   Year _____   Pages _____

Memorable Quote	Page Number

Characters

Plot Summary

Notes

Rating ☆ ☆ ☆ ☆ ☆

Book Title _____

Author _____ Nationality _____

Genre _____ Year _____ Pages _____

Memorable Quote	Page Number

Characters

Plot Summary

Notes

Rating ☆ ☆ ☆ ☆ ☆

Book Title _____

Author _____ Nationality _____

Genre _____ Year _____ Pages _____

Memorable Quote	Page Number

Characters

Plot Summary

Notes

Rating ☆ ☆ ☆ ☆ ☆

Book Title _____

Author _____   Nationality _____

Genre _____   Year _____   Pages _____

Memorable Quote	Page Number

Characters

Plot Summary

Notes

Rating ☆ ☆ ☆ ☆ ☆

Book Title _____

Author _____ Nationality _____

Genre _____ Year _____ Pages _____

Memorable Quote	Page Number

Characters

Plot Summary

Notes

Rating ☆ ☆ ☆ ☆ ☆

Book Title _____

Author _____   Nationality _____

Genre _____   Year _____   Pages _____

Memorable Quote	Page Number

Characters

Plot Summary

Notes

Rating ☆ ☆ ☆ ☆ ☆

Book Title _____

Author _____   Nationality _____

Genre _____   Year _____   Pages _____

Memorable Quote	Page Number

Characters

Plot Summary

Notes

Rating ☆ ☆ ☆ ☆ ☆

Book Title _____

Author _____ Nationality _____

Genre _____ Year _____ Pages _____

Memorable Quote	Page Number

Characters

Plot Summary

Notes

Rating ☆ ☆ ☆ ☆ ☆

Book Title _____

Author _____   Nationality _____

Genre _____   Year _____   Pages _____

Memorable Quote	Page Number

Characters

Plot Summary

Notes

Rating ☆ ☆ ☆ ☆ ☆

Book Title

Author _____   Nationality _____

Genre _____   Year _____   Pages _____

Memorable Quote	Page Number

Characters

Plot Summary

Notes

Rating ☆ ☆ ☆ ☆ ☆

Book Title

Author _____   Nationality _____

Genre _____   Year _____   Pages _____

Memorable Quote	Page Number

Characters

Plot Summary

Notes

Rating ☆ ☆ ☆ ☆ ☆

Book Title _____

Author _____ Nationality _____

Genre _____ Year _____ Pages _____

Memorable Quote	Page Number

Characters

Plot Summary

Notes

Rating ☆ ☆ ☆ ☆ ☆

Book Title _____

Author _____   Nationality _____

Genre _____   Year _____   Pages _____

Memorable Quote	Page Number

Characters

Plot Summary

Notes

Rating ☆ ☆ ☆ ☆ ☆

Book Title _____

Author _____   Nationality _____

Genre _____   Year _____   Pages _____

Memorable Quote	Page Number

Characters

Plot Summary

Notes

Rating ☆ ☆ ☆ ☆ ☆

Book Title _____

Author _____   Nationality _____

Genre _____   Year _____   Pages _____

Memorable Quote	Page Number

Characters

Plot Summary

Notes

Rating ☆ ☆ ☆ ☆ ☆

Book Title _____

Author _____ Nationality _____

Genre _____ Year _____ Pages _____

Memorable Quote	Page Number

Characters

Plot Summary

Notes

Rating ☆ ☆ ☆ ☆ ☆

Book Title _____

Author _____ Nationality _____

Genre _____ Year _____ Pages _____

Memorable Quote	Page Number

Characters

Plot Summary

Notes

Rating ☆ ☆ ☆ ☆ ☆

Book Title _____

Author _____   Nationality _____

Genre _____   Year _____   Pages _____

Memorable Quote	Page Number

Characters

Plot Summary

Notes

Rating ☆ ☆ ☆ ☆ ☆

Book Title

Author _____   Nationality _____

Genre _____   Year _____   Pages _____

Memorable Quote	Page Number

Characters

Plot Summary

Notes

Rating ☆ ☆ ☆ ☆ ☆

Book Title

Author _____   Nationality _____

Genre _____   Year _____   Pages _____

Memorable Quote	Page Number

Characters

Plot Summary

Notes

Rating ☆ ☆ ☆ ☆ ☆

Book Title _____

Author _____ Nationality _____

Genre _____ Year _____ Pages _____

Memorable Quote	Page Number

Characters

Plot Summary

Notes

Rating ☆ ☆ ☆ ☆ ☆

Book Title _____

Author _____   Nationality _____

Genre _____   Year _____   Pages _____

Memorable Quote	Page Number

Characters

Plot Summary

Notes

Rating ☆ ☆ ☆ ☆ ☆

Book Title _____

Author _____   Nationality _____

Genre _____   Year _____   Pages _____

Memorable Quote	Page Number

Characters

Plot Summary

Notes

Rating ☆ ☆ ☆ ☆ ☆

Book Title

Author _____   Nationality _____

Genre _____   Year _____   Pages _____

Memorable Quote	Page Number

Characters

Plot Summary

Notes

Rating ☆ ☆ ☆ ☆ ☆

Book Title _____

Author _____ Nationality _____

Genre _____ Year _____ Pages _____

Memorable Quote	Page Number

Characters

Plot Summary

Notes

Rating ☆ ☆ ☆ ☆ ☆

Book Title _____

Author _____   Nationality _____

Genre _____   Year _____   Pages _____

Memorable Quote	Page Number

Characters

Plot Summary

Notes

Rating ☆ ☆ ☆ ☆ ☆

Book Title

Author _____ Nationality _____

Genre _____ Year _____ Pages _____

Memorable Quote	Page Number

Characters

Plot Summary

Notes

Rating ☆ ☆ ☆ ☆ ☆

Book Title _____

Author _____   Nationality _____

Genre _____   Year _____   Pages _____

Memorable Quote	Page Number

Characters

Plot Summary

Notes

Rating ☆ ☆ ☆ ☆ ☆

Book Title _____

Author _____   Nationality _____

Genre _____   Year _____   Pages _____

Memorable Quote	Page Number

Characters

Plot Summary

Notes

Rating ☆ ☆ ☆ ☆ ☆

Book Title _____

Author _____   Nationality _____

Genre _____   Year _____   Pages _____

Memorable Quote	Page Number

Characters

Plot Summary

Notes

Rating ☆ ☆ ☆ ☆ ☆

Book Title _____

Author _____   Nationality _____

Genre _____   Year _____   Pages _____

Memorable Quote	Page Number

Characters

Plot Summary

Notes

Rating ☆ ☆ ☆ ☆ ☆

Book Title _____

Author _____ Nationality _____

Genre _____ Year _____ Pages _____

Memorable Quote	Page Number

Characters

Plot Summary

Notes

Rating ☆ ☆ ☆ ☆ ☆

Book Title _____

Author _____   Nationality _____

Genre _____   Year _____   Pages _____

Memorable Quote	Page Number

Characters

Plot Summary

Notes

Rating ☆ ☆ ☆ ☆ ☆

Book Title

Author _____   Nationality _____

Genre _____   Year _____   Pages _____

Memorable Quote	Page Number

Characters

Plot Summary

Notes

Rating ☆ ☆ ☆ ☆ ☆

Book Title

Author _____   Nationality _____

Genre _____   Year _____   Pages _____

Memorable Quote	Page Number

Characters

Plot Summary

Notes

Rating ☆ ☆ ☆ ☆ ☆

Book Title

Author _____ Nationality _____

Genre _____ Year _____ Pages _____

Memorable Quote	Page Number

Characters

Plot Summary

Notes

Rating ☆ ☆ ☆ ☆ ☆

Book Title _____

Author _____   Nationality _____

Genre _____   Year _____   Pages _____

Memorable Quote	Page Number

Characters

Plot Summary

Notes

Rating ☆ ☆ ☆ ☆ ☆

100 Must-Read (Fiction) Books

- Harry Potter and the Philosopher's Stone — J.K. Rowling
- The Hunger Games — Suzanne Collins
- The BFG — Roald Dahl
- The Very Hungry Caterpillar — Eric Carle
- Winnie-the-Pooh — A. A. Milne
- The Cat in the Hat — Dr Seuss
- The Lord of the Rings: The Fellowship of the Ring — J.R.R. Tolkien
- Charlotte's Web — E.B. White
- Northern Lights — Philip Pullman
- The Lion, the Witch and the Wardrobe — C.S Lewis
- Flour Babies — Anne Fine
- Private Peaceful — Sir Michael Morpurgo
- Journey to the River Sea — Eva Ibbotson
- Millions — Frank Cottrell Boyce
- Matilda — Roald Dahl
- Once — Morris Gleitzman
- The Story of Tracy Beaker — Jacqueline Wilson
- Skellig — David Almond
- Artemis Fowl — Eoin Colfer
- Carrie's War — Nina Bawden
- Goodnight Mister Tom — Michelle Magorian
- The Borrowers — Mary Norton
- The Hobbit — J.R.R. Tolkien
- Stig of the Dump — Clive King
- The Adventures of Tintin — Hergé
- Swallows and Amazons — Arthur Ransome
- Ballet Shoes — Noel Streatfeild

- The Little Prince — Antoine de Saint-Exupery
- The Wolves of Willoughby Chase — Joan Aiken
- The Witches — Roald Dahl
- Truckers — Terry Pratchett
- Holes — Louis Sachar
- A Monster Calls — Patrick Ness
- The Absolutely True Diary of a Part-Time Indian — Sherman Alexie
- The Book Thief — Markus Zusak
- A Wrinkle in Time — Madeliene L'Engle
- The Outsiders — S.E. Hinton
- Phantom Tollbooth — Norton Juster
- The Giver — Lois Lowry
- Are You There God? It's Me, Margaret — Judy Blume
- To Kill a Mockingbird — Harper Lee
- Roll of Thunder, Hear My Cry — Mildred D. Taylor
- Anne of Green Gables — Lucy Maud Montgomery
- The Chronicles of Narnia — C.S. Lewis
- Monster — Walter Dean Myers
- The Golden Compass — Philip Pullman
- The Diary of a Young Girl — Anne Frank
- From the Mixed-Up Files of Mrs. Basil E. Frankweiler — E. L. Konigsburg
- Looking for Alaska — John Green
- The Curious Incident of the Dog in the Night-Time — Mark Haddon
- Little House on the Prairie — Laura Ingalls Wilder
- The Miraculous Journey of Edward Tulane — Kate DiCamillo
- Wonder — R. J. Palacio
- The Sword in the Stone — T.H. White
- The Catcher in the Rye — J.D. Salinger
- Little Women — Louisa May Alcott

- The Adventures of Huckleberry Finn — Mark Twain
- The Wonderful Wizard of Oz — L. Frank Baum
- Lord of the Flies — William Golding
- Charlie and the Chocolate Factory — Roald Dahl
- Alice's Adventures in Wonderland — Lewis Carroll
- Bridge to Terabithia — Katherine Paterson
- The Call of the Wild — Jack London
- A Separate Peace — John Knowles
- Harriet the Spy — Louise Fitzhugh
- The Chocolate War — Robert Cormier
- Jacob Have I Loved — Katherine Paterson
- A Series of Unfortunate Events Series — Lemony Snicket
- Hatchet — Cary Paulsen
- Feed — M.T. Anderson
- The Alchemyst — Michael Scott
- The Princess Bride — William Goldman
- Beezus and Ramona — Beverly Cleary
- Tarzan of the Apes — Edgar Rice Burroughs
- Johnny Tremain — Esther Forbes
- The Westing Game — Ellen Raskin
- The Wind in the Willows — Kenneth Grahame
- Speak — Laurie Halse Anderson
- Mary Poppins — P. L. Travers
- The Fault in Our Stars — John Green
- A Northern Light — Jennifer Donnelly
- The Yearling — Marjorie Kinnan Rawlings
- For Freedom — Kimberly Brubaker Bradley
- The Wall: Growing Up Behind the Iron Curtain — Peter Sis
- The Illustrated Man — Ray Bradbury
- A Wreath for Emmett Till — Marilyn Nelson

- Every Day – David Levithan
- Where Things Come Back – John Corey Whaley
- Number the Stars – Lois Lowry
- Blankets – Craig Thompson
- Private Peaceful – Michael Morpurgo
- The Witch of Blackbird Pond – Elizabeth George Speare
- Dangerous Angels – Francesca Lia Block
- Frindle – Andrew Clements
- Boxers and Saints – Gene Luen Yang
- The Graveyard Book – Neil Gaiman
- City of Beasts – Isabel Allende
- American Born Chinese – Gene Luen Yang
- The Lost Conspiracy – Frances Hardinge
- Dogsbody – Diana Wynne Jones

NOTES